MW01110043

The 7 Secrets To Create Your Fate

Sharmen R. Lane

Bloomington, IN Milton Keynes, UK

authorHOUSE®

AuthorHouse™
1663 Liberty Drive, Suite 200
Bloomington, IN 47403
www.authorhouse.com
Phone: 1-800-839-8640

AuthorHouse™ UK Ltd.
500 Avebury Boulevard
Central Milton Keynes, MK9 2BE
www.authorhouse.co.uk
Phone: 08001974150

First published by AuthorHouse 2/12/2007

ISBN: 978-1-4259-8859-3 (sc)
ISBN: 978-1-4259-8861-6 (e)

Printed in the United States of America
Bloomington, Indiana

This book is printed on acid-free paper.

Dedication

This book is dedicated to all the people who have come in and out of my life. I have learned something from each and every one of you. Every experience-good, bad or indifferent-has made me who I am today.

I believe people come into your life for a season, a reason, or a lifetime. I am thankful for every one of them.

I want to give a special thank you to my grandmother, Joyce Lane. You have a heart that gives more unconditional love than anyone I have ever met. You are beautiful inside and out and in every way possible. I hope someday to have even half of your grace. You have impacted my life in more ways than I will ever be able to explain. I love you.

Contents

Introduction

Congratulations and thank you for joining me on taking your first step to an extraordinary life. It takes an incredible person to wake up one day and say "I want more. I want to be more, I want to do more, I want to have more."

I am not only going to motivate you to get what you want, I am going to inspire you to go out and get it now! Most things that motivate us wear off a few days after doing them. But when you are inspired it becomes a part of who you are forever. It is like a flame burning inside you that can't be put out.

Most of us sit back and wait for the miraculous to happen. Let me be the first to tell you, we make our own miracles. If you do nothing I guarantee that you will get the same in return... absolutely nothing.

What you get out of life is directly related to what you put into it. You bought this book and you are reading it. That, in and of itself, puts you in the driver's seat to making extraordinary things happen for you. Most people don't even do that much. Surveys have shown that 90% of people who purchase a program like this never even crack open the cover. You are reading this so you are already well on your way to creating your fate.

So here's my story...

I've been a student of psychology for over 20 years. I've read every book, heard every tape, been to every seminar and workshop, and have seen more therapists than I care to admit.

All of us had something about our childhood that we didn't like or wish had been different. It's all relative. What was awful to you or I may have only been the tip of the iceberg to someone else or vice versa. This book is about taking whatever your life experience has been and using it to get what you want now.

My childhood was what it was. Some parts were good, some parts were bad and others were indifferent. Teenage life rolled around, and in the 7th grade my school psychologist approached me after I had given a required "me" speech in health class and asked if I wanted to be a peer counselor. I had to do some extra reading, training, classes, testing, etc. Something inside me said this is what I was meant to do. And a peer counselor I became.

Then came high school. Middle of my junior year I moved to a new city and new school where I knew no one. This was where I took peer counseling and psychology to a higher level. I read and studied everything I could get my hands on.

I ended up dropping out of high school with only one semester left. I later realized that wasn't such a smart move so I got my GED but figured out that it really isn't the same as a high school diploma, so I went to night school and got my actual high school diploma. To this day I am still a student currently working on my psychology and communications degrees with full intentions of getting more because I love to learn.

Then I became an adult doing lots of different jobs looking for the one that was truly fulfilling. In my mid twenties I was in a job that I didn't love but didn't hate. I was a sales rep for a wholesale mortgage lender. I continued to do it, day after day, month after month, year after year for about ten years.

I continued to make more and more money. Every year I would make more money than the last. That doesn't sound so bad, right? One year I made slightly over a million dollars. That January, I made over one hundred thousand dollars that ONE MONTH!!!! And that year I made one million two hundred thousand dollars. That is the year that I started to think of quitting. Yep that's right, quitting. Who does that???

Who leaves a seven figure a year job? You have no idea how many people asked me that question when I told them I was thinking of leaving the mortgage business that I had been in for over ten years and made damn near a fortune at.

"What? Are you crazy? Why would you leave a job like that?" Both are things I heard countless times. My answer was always the same. "I've wanted to write a book for as long as I can remember. It's time for me to live my passion." When I was seven or eight years old I remember coloring in a Yogi Bear coloring book that had a little sentence at the bottom of each page. I told my mom that I was going to take those one line sentences and make a storybook out of it.

Regardless, everyone I told that I was leaving my extremely well paying job would give me that puzzled confused look that was quickly followed by "Why do you want to leave a seven figure a year job to write a book? Why don't you just do this business? You are clearly good at it."

So I asked myself that question everyday for the next 12 months. Why do I want to leave a good job that provides a phenomenal lifestyle, is easy and I'm good at? So I asked myself this question, "What do I do?" I do loans. I'm in sales for a wholesale mortgage lender. I've done this job for years. I'm no longer challenged. I could do higher volume of loans, but that is just more of the same. I don't love what I do anymore and I'm not growing or learning or accomplishing anything. So that was it. I no longer had passion for the job I spend ten plus hours a day at. The next day I quit.

Then the real pessimists and crazy makers came out. I would talk to people that I had worked with who would tell me other people (of course no one was going admit it was really them) thought I was stupid. Yes, that's right stupid. Stupid! I was being called stupid. Now, I have been called many things in my life, but stupid was not one of them.

One person (and if he is reading this, you know who you are) said, "What makes you think you have the credibility or authority to write a book. Who do you think you are?" Hhmmmmm. "Good question," I thought. Here I am jobless, and I'm getting doubt from people I thought were friends. You are probably thinking, "With friends like that who needs enemies." I wondered the same thing.

For the next several months I wrote in my journal, studied, read, researched and practiced everything I knew. I wrote down every thought, every idea. I put on paper all the things I knew and had lived, learned and taught over the last 20 years.

Now I'm sharing all that research, education and experience to inspire everyone I can to live their passion and be, do, and have more than they ever thought possible. The pages you are about to read will empower you to do what you love, find your passion and...Create Your Fate.

Chapter One

Knowin where you're goin

The first step to create your fate is "Knowin where you're goin." Sounds silly to say, doesn't it? I thought so too, as soon as I wrote it. Then I got to thinking. What do I have to do to create my fate? The first thing that came to mind was, if I want to create anything I first have to know what I want.

I think this is a major problem for most of us. How often do you hear people complain, "I'm not happy." Or, I want to do something different or have something more, but we don't know what that "something" is. Perhaps, you are bored with your life, but you don't know what you would rather be doing. That is the first thing you have to decide.

The definition of fate is: "The supposed force, principle, or power that predetermines events." If there is some force or power that determines my fate, I'm going to decide what it is. That's why the name of this book is The 7 Secrets to Create Your Fate. There are 7 chapters in this book, each one giving you a secret on how to create your fate.

It is your job to decide what happens to you. Life is usually what happens to us when we aren't paying attention. If you want your goals to happen, you must take a moment to think about what you want. Do you want a different job, different lifestyle, or a better relationship with your spouse or kids? Do you want more income, a new home or a new car? What do you want?

While you are thinking about what you want, forget about reality and think fantasy! Take reality out of it. I'm sure you've heard the phrase…"Reality Sucks." Well, we get to choose our own reality. So if reality sucks, you have no one to blame but yourself. It is up to you to create a better reality. If you are going to dream then dream big. Why be realistic? You can be, do, or have whatever you want. Who decides what is realistic anyway? Is it your parents, society, your boss? If you were going to let someone else decide your fate you would not be reading this book.

This is the first part to create your fate. You have to know what you want before you can go out and get it. Once you know that, you can MAP it. But before we get to MAPing, you must identify the things you want to be, do, and have. So, this is your first action item. I call it an action item because you are creating movement in your life. And what starts movement…action.

Grab a piece of paper and write down all the areas of your life that you are not satisfied with. Little or big, important or silly, just write them down. Basically, what are you complaining about? What are you constantly telling yourself you don't want? Here is an example of what this looks like.

I hate my life. I hate everything about it. I don't like my job. I don't like my boss. I don't like my home, I don't like my clothes, or my hair, or my shoes, or my car, or my level of education, or level of success, or my checking account balance, I hate everything. Just let 'er rip.

Forget that your mother told you to never say "hate." This isn't about being nice or polite or proper. This is about using words with power to get you to do something about it. If you simply say you don't like something or "well, I wish things were a little different" you are never going to do anything about it. So to heck with what anyone else thinks. Just write.

Look at me. I had a job that I made a ton of money at. Anytime I told someone that I didn't love my life or said I wanted something different, inevitably someone would say, "SHUT UP!! What are you complaining about??? You make a million dollars a year!" So, of course, I would stop complaining and continue to do the same thing day in and day out.

But ya know what? It's not up to everyone else to decide that what I have is enough. No one else can decide that I can't have something more or something different. I wanted to live my passion, do what I love AND make a million dollars a year. What's wrong with that? Now you may be thinking "that makes you crazy and greedy!" If that is anywhere close to a thought you had then you need to rethink what you believe in. Say this out loud, "WHAT I BELIEVE IS WHAT I'LL RECEIVE."

Do you believe the universe is full of endless opportunities? Or do you believe the world is full of limits and boundaries? There are no limits! The only limits to what you can be, do or have are the ones that you create in your own head.

Think about this. Where would we be if Thomas Edison decided a candle was as good as it got? We wouldn't have light bulbs. How would we travel if the Wright brothers hadn't invented the airplane? Or better yet, what if Dr. Hans von Ohain and Sir Frank Whittle decided that propeller plane was the only way to fly? We wouldn't have jet engine airplanes. How would we talk to people anywhere in the world if Alexander Graham Bell decided the only way to communicate with people far away was by mail and nothing else was possible? We wouldn't have the telephone. All these are examples of people who believed something that didn't exist yet, was possible.

If you believe that there are no possibilities beyond what you already are, do or have, then you may as well stop living. What's the point in living if you've done all there is to do or have all there is to have? There is always something more. If you have your bachelor degree, go get your master's. If you already have your master's, go get your doctorate. If you have your doctorate, go get another one. If you make a million go make two. You should always be learning, doing, growing, and achieving.

So get busy! What are you waiting for? Start writing! Write down everything in your life that you are not happy with. Unfortunately, as a whole, the majority of people find more power in the negative side of things. If someone gives you a compliment it is usually quickly dismissed. But if someone says something nasty, we can fuss and fume about it for hours, sometimes even days or weeks. When did you last receive a compliment and you marveled in it for days? That is why it is best to write down what you are not happy with. It is a great starting point to lead the way to getting what you want.

I don't know about you, but I find peace in clarity. Maybe you're feeling down and depressed but you don't really know why. You have a job, spouse, home, money, kids. You have what looks like a happy life, but, for some reason, you just aren't happy. You are lacking that gusto, that juice, that "get up in the morning and charge into the day with passion and excitement" attitude. Perhaps that's because something is missing. Deep down inside, you know what that "something" is. I hope you know by identifying that "thing" and by writing it down you will create a happier more passionate life.

Perhaps your situation is the exact opposite. You live paycheck to paycheck, have a job that you hate or no job at all. You rent an apartment that you do not like or your relationship is not what you want it to be. Believe it or not, I've been there. I had a job that was okay, an apartment that was just average and a life that was nothing special. If any of these or something similar is where you find yourself day in and day out, then the first action item was probably a simple one. You probably know which parts of your life you are unhappy with. Just write them down.

I have done this exercise with many people. I've done it on me many times.

Years ago, I was a secretary. I didn't love it, didn't hate it. I lived in a studio apartment, and made about $30,000 a year and that was including overtime and bonuses. One day I wrote down all the things I wasn't happy with and what I wanted instead. The next thing I knew I got a job as a salesperson at a mortgage company and over the next 8 years I made over 4 million dollars. I had bought several cars and several houses. Life seemed pretty good. Everything I had wanted, I wrote down, made a plan and got it. I had a job that paid unbelievably well. I had fabulous house, nice car, great income, good friends, good job, plenty of freedom and lots of flexibility.

For those 8 years I was climbing the ladder of success, at least what my version of success was at the time. I was continually learning or achieving or doing something that I had never done before. Over time I became complacent. I stopped growing. I wasn't nearly as challenged at my job as I had once been. But hey, I made great money so why change.

Slowly but surely I became less and less happy. I was less and less excited about waking up in the morning and taking on the day. Finally it got to a point where everyday I struggled to get out of bed. I could not figure out what my problem was. I had this "perfect" life, or at least it looked perfect, but I wasn't fulfilled. I felt empty. Why? That is what I had to figure out.

So, I dragged myself out of bed, grabbed a piece of paper and here's what I wrote. "I hate my job. I make a ton of money but I'm not challenged, I'm not learning, I'm not growing. I'm bored, stagnant, and unchallenged." Boy was that hard to write. But, it felt great to be honest. I felt as if a 300 pound gorilla was lifted off my shoulders and I was about to have a breakthrough.

I read over what I had just written. Then I thought, "Okay, now I know what I'm not happy with." That's good. At least I know why I feel the way I do. Now what? So I thought, just for kicks and giggles, let's write down everything I want to be, do, and have. I made several columns and put each aspect of my life in each one. I had a column for dream job, family, money, travel, and self. Just in case you were wondering, when I had done this list 8 years earlier I had only written things relating to my career. I wrote that my dream job made lots of money, had freedom and flexibility. All of which I got. So now it's 8 years later and time to redefine what I want in my life.

Below are my lists:

Job	Family	Travel	Money	Self
Author	husband	Europe	limitless	psych degree
Flex hrs	children	Tropics	7+ figures	Comm degree
Growth	close	East Coast		learning
Creative	loving			Help others
Teach	sharing			22% body fat
Train	supportive			feel great

This is your second action item, which I found to be much more exciting to do and a lot more fun! By now you have written at least one thing in your life that you are unhappy or unsatisfied with. Now, think about everything you want in its place. Things you want to do, places you want to go, the job you want to have, the life you want to live, the relationship of your dreams, etc., etc., etc. You might have one thing or a long list of things. Either way, you now get to have a little fun.

Grab another blank piece of paper and a pen. Starting with the first item, write what you want in its place. If you wrote that you were unsatisfied with your job, write down what your dream job would be. How would it feel, what hours would you work, what would it look like, where would it be, how much would it pay, etc.?

The most important thing here is to throw all reason, rational and reality out the window. This is not a reality job it is your dream job. Or perhaps you are looking for the man or woman of your dreams. That's okay too. Write down everything you want that person to have. What would he/she look like, what would you do together, where would you go together, what goals would he/she have and what would your goals be together?

This is you identifying what it is that you want. Don't worry about how you are going to get it or ask if it even exists. Just take this opportunity to find out for yourself what it is that you really want. Have fun with it. Write down all the thoughts and ideas you have for your perfect job, spouse, home, car, education, etc. If you wrote down more than one thing that you are unsatisfied with, now write down what you want in place of each item.

That's it. At this point you should have written down what you don't like about your life and what you do want in its place. That my friends, is Knowing Where You're Goin!

Sharmen R. Lane

Notes: What did I get out of this chapter? What do I want to remember? Etc.

_____

_____

_____

_____

_____

_____

_____

_____

_____

_____

_____

_____

_____

_____

_____

_____

_____

Chapter Two

MAP'in For Your Passion

Now you know where you want to go, it's time to figure out how to get there. This is what you do after you're Knowin Where Your Goin. MAP stands for *MAKE-A-PLAN*. Just knowing where you want to go, won't get you there. Look over your list and find one item that you want to start on. This is the item that you are going to MAP.

MAPing is very important because there are certain things that need to be done in order for you to accomplish your goal, and you need to find out what those "things" are. Just like you would need a road atlas or a map or a direction website to give you step by step directions to arrive at a specific location. You need to get the step-by-step directions that will lead you to your goal.

Years ago, I was a secretary and was making 30K a year. I decided I wanted to go into sales. I had worked for MCI in the business sales department a few years before and even the worst sales people made a lot more money than I did. So, I decided that being in sales was where the money was.

I took a job at a mortgage company, again as a secretary and again working with their sales department.

And yet again, everyone I worked with was making more money than I. While I was doing my secretarial duties I listened, studied and learned everything I could about the mortgage business. Just about a year later I took the leap of faith.

I was hired as a sales rep at another mortgage company. As I mentioned before I had written a list for my dream job and on it was a six figure+ income, flexibility and freedom. That is exactly what my new sales job had. I was an outside sales rep and as long as I produced a minimum amount of sales, no one bothered me. I could do my job from the beach if I wanted and as long as my numbers came in, that was all that mattered. I spent the next 8 years as a sales rep in the mortgage business. This is truly where I learned all about MAPing. Not only did I Make-A-Plan for my yearly goals, but I made monthly, weekly and daily goals as well.

Let me give you an everyday example of why it is important to Make A Plan. It's Christmas time and you're grocery shopping for your holiday dinner. You run into a friend from high school whom you haven't seen in years. She tells you that she's married with 2 wonderful children and they just bought their first home and are having a Christmas/ Housewarming party next Friday.

She gives you the address and says "Please come, I'd love for you to meet my family." You say "Sure, I wouldn't miss it."

A few days go by and you look at your calendar and realize tonight is your high school pal's party. You have her address and you get in your car. Do you drive around aimlessly all around town until you just so happen to run into your friends house? Is that likely to happen? You just drive around to accidentally stumble into exactly what you were looking for. Not really.

If you want to go to this party you better find a way to get there. You'd likely call to get directions, or look at a map, or in today's world go online to some direction or map website. My point is, if something as simple as driving to a specific location requires thought and preparation, wouldn't you think arriving at your dream goal would require a MAP too?

Since we're on the topic of directions, do you ever wish you had an instruction booklet that came with the person you are married to or are in a relationship with? I'm sure you are nodding your head. People are fascinating creatures. The next time you are having a problem how about asking for a MAP.

Men, do you get frustrated when your wife or girlfriend is having a meltdown? Most of us know men are typically more logical and women are typically more emotional. You have no idea what to do, or whatever you are doing is making matters worse. Stop for a moment and ask yourself this question, "Do I want to make this better?" If the answer is yes, then be honest. Say "Honey I have no idea what you are needing from me right now. Please tell me. Give me directions. Give me instructions so I can do it right?" You will save your-self a lot of trial and error and a lot of time and energy. If you do what she tells you she needs you to do, you will be her hero. Ladies, you can do the same for your man. If you don't know what to do to fix a situation, ask. AAhhh, a MAP, a set of step by step instructions to handle your partner in the best way possible. What a concept!

Figuring out what you want is the first step you need to take to get what you want. After you have determined what you want, make a plan.

January 1ST every year, I write what I want to ac-complish. I also do something a bit more fun. I do what is called a "visual map." I'm grateful to my thera-pist, Jenny England, who taught me what a visual map is and its importance.

A visual map is similar to a collage. Gather pic-tures of the things you want to do, be, have, or all of the above. For example, a couple of years ago I came up with the title for my first book. I then took the back cover of a famous author's book and put my picture over hers and put my own bio on it.

I did the same thing for the front cover of a Time magazine. I also took the cover of an Oprah magazine and put a picture of myself with the title of my book under my photo and wrote an endorsement from Oprah right next to it. I took letters from several headlines of all different colors and shapes and sizes and spelled the title of my book at the very top of the poster board.

I did this with every aspect of my life. I wanted to get to my happy weight of 115 pounds and get leaner than I had ever been before. So I cut out pictures of legs that looked the way I wanted mine to look. I did the same for biceps, triceps, shoulders, abs, and buns.

Then I found pictures of my dream house and dream yard and dream dog. I gathered pictures of places I wanted to go and things I wanted to see. I even gathered romantic pictures of couples that looked the way I wanted to be with my spouse. Being as I didn't have a spouse, I found pictures of what I want him to be like when I find him. Then I found pictures of how we would look and things we would do together.

I printed a picture of a check and filled it in with my name and signed it as if it were from a publisher. Everything I wanted I found a picture for and glued it to my visual map.

The moral of the story is... Don't underestimate the power of pictures. Anyone who knows anything about memory techniques will tell you that if you want to remember something, visualize it as a picture. I'm sure you've seen someone whose face you know but you forgot their name. That's because the face is a picture in your mind but the name is not. The name is heard, not seen.

What would you think of if I asked you to describe your car, the one you have or the one you want? You wouldn't think of the letters that spell H-O-N-D-A or F-E-R-R-A-R-I. You would think of what it looks like and describe it visually.

Of course, you don't get to simply cut out pictures and glue them onto poster board and forget about them while the arts and crafts fairies go to work. You have pictures for what you want. Now write what has to be done in order to get it.

The best example I think most people can relate to is that of weight loss. Almost every adult, at least in the US, has been on a diet. First off, I don't generally like words that begin with die, and I don't like the term "lose weight." These don't work for me is because anytime you lose something you try to find it. You lost a check, you look for it. You lost your keys, you look for them. If you willingly give something away, it is gone, never to be seen again. So if you see this as something you have lost, then logically you try to find it again. I believe most people who have lost weight prefer it to be gone forever.

This is what I did. I identified how much I wanted to weigh instead of identifying how much I wanted to "lose." I decided on the body fat percentage I wanted to be and found photos of what I wanted my body to look like.

Once again, this is just clarifying what I want. How do I get to be 115 pounds and 22% body fat? First thing is to get a membership to a gym. Then after having an evaluation of my current physical status, come to find out I was at 35% body fat (yikes), I decided I couldn't do it on my own because everything I had been doing for the last 25 years clearly hadn't worked. So, I hired a trainer and saw a nutritionist.

Then my trainer and I came up with a plan for how often I would workout with her to do weight training, how much cardiovascular exercise I needed to do per week and how many calories I could consume per day and the types of foods I could eat in order to achieve my goal.

That is MAPing. I had to Make-A-Plan in order to get to where I wanted to be, because it certainly wasn't going to happen all by itself.

I did the same thing when I was working for the mortgage company as a sales rep. Every year on New Year's Day I would write out my career goals for the year. In order to achieve that goal I needed to break it down into small, doable pieces. This step is called dicing. Breaking down what needs to be done into simple, bite size, easy to digest, pieces.

So, I looked at what I wanted to accomplish and broke it down into what I needed to do per month. Then I broke the month down by what needed to be done each week. Inevitably, I followed the weekly with what needed to be done daily in order to ultimately arrive at my year end goal.

I did this process 6 out of 8 years and guess how many times I hit my goal. You got it... 6! "What happened the other 2 years", I'm sure you are wondering. They were my last 2 years in the mortgage business and I was making other goals to do other things, like writing the book that you are now reading!

In the mortgage business there are certain things that are statistically true. For instance, about half of the loans that come in the door will end up funding in any one month. Therefore, I needed to bring in twice the number of loans than what I wanted to close. So, I would take my yearly goal and divide it by 12. This is how many loans I needed to close on average each month. Each month, I'd take that number and divide it by the number of business days in the month. Then I would multiply by 2 which would tell me how many loans I needed to bring in every day.

You can use this same formula to get to a goal weight. How many pounds lighter would you like to be and by when? Let's say I want to be 10 pounds lighter in the next 30 days. Take the number of pounds and multiply by 3,500. In this case it would be 35,000. For those of you who don't know, it takes 3,500 calories to burn one pound of fat.

Now take the 35,000 calories and divide it by 30 and you'd come up with 1,166. This means that you would have to eat 1,166 fewer calories per day, burn 1166 calories more than you eat per day, or eat about 583 calories less and burn 583 calories more in order to get to your goal weight.

Being 10 pounds lighter in 30 days may sound a little tough. Consuming 35,000 fewer calories or burning 35,000 more calories in one month may also sound tough. Eating 500ish calories less a day and burning about 500 calories more a day should seem a whole lot easier.

Hopefully, by now you can see the importance of MAPing. You don't just wake up one day and magically appear at your goal. You figure out what you want, you Make A Plan, then dice it up into daily bite size pieces. Then you are able to work toward your goal in small measurable little accomplishments. Every time you accomplish a little piece, you are given the motivation to stick to your goal and work on the next little piece. This way every day you feel as though you have accomplished something. Every day you have something to be proud of. Every day you will be one step closer to what you want.

So what was it that you wanted to be, do or have? Write down the things that need to be done in order to achieve it. Then dice it up and assign one little bit of action for every day. You will quickly be on your way to your new fate!

Let's not forget the importance of rewards. Every time you accomplish one of your steps, do something that makes you feel fantastic! I love spa treatments. So every time I got 5 pounds closer to my feel good weight I would plan a spa day. I would get a manicure, pedicure and a massage. Every time I wanted to dive into the Krispy Kreme's I would think about how icky I would feel with all that sugar and lard coursing through my veins. I would also think about which I wanted more. Do I want the donut or do I want to be even closer to my happy weight and a full luxurious day of pampering? I'm sure you can guess which one I chose far more often.

Don't think the donut never won. It did. However, when I had my goal in site, staying on the path to what I wanted was a far more powerful force. So if you have a little set back, just let it go and start fresh the next day. Things are much easier to accomplish when the end is in sight. Every day you will have a little goal and every day you get to feel fabulous because you are one step closer to what you want. What a way to live… Every day with a sense of accomplishment!

Rewarding yourself for a job well done is amazingly effective and tremendously useful. What makes you feel good? Is it a night out with your significant other, a walk in park, going to the movies, a spa day, a manicure, a new pair of shoes, poker with the guys, weekend in Vegas? Give yourself a reward and do it often. There is nothing that makes you stay on track with your goal than doing little things along the way that reinforce your positive behavior.

When you are setting your goals and MAP'ing and dicing them, set the landmarks with the points at which you get your reward. In the beginning it is very important to reward yourself early and often. I know this will sound silly but when I lost a percent of body fat I would buy a new pair of shoes. I love shoes! I chose this as my reward because size 7 shoes always fit. I didn't care if I had to go to a 7 and a half. I didn't want to put on my skinny jeans because I wasn't at my full goal yet. I wanted to feel good about the progress I had made and not feel discouraged because the size jeans that I ultimately wanted to get into still didn't fit. It is very important to do something that rewards your progress and keeps you on the right track.

To make your plan, write down what needs to be done, break it up into simple steps, and dice those steps up into tiny bite size daily tasks. And that is your MAP.

Notes: What did I get out of this chapter? What do I want to remember? Etc.

_____

_____

_____

_____

_____

_____

_____

_____

_____

_____

_____

_____

_____

_____

_____

_____

_____

Chapter Three

Passion Equals Action

Have you ever been so passionate about something that it seems as if you were born to do it, have it or be it? I can say that I have and I truly believe that when you follow your passion, everything simply falls into place.

I had my first experience speaking in front of a group when I was in the 5th grade. At least it is the first one I remember. We had to do a science project in front of the class and have visual aids. My project was on the brain. I remember being nervous and practicing in front of the mirror for hours. The day came and my little science project went really well. I walked away after my report and thought "Wow, that was cool." Most everyone else in my class hated the experience. There I was 10 years old and I thought it was fun.

Then a few years later, junior high rolled around. The school psychologist, Mr. Stanforth went to every health class and made every student stand up in front of the whole class and talk about themselves for a full 10 minutes.

One weekend I wrote out exactly what I was going to say. Then I memorized it and got it down pat. Monday morning the question was asked who wants to go first. That was a question rarely anyone raised a hand to, but that day I raised mine. As I walked to the front of the class, my heart was pounding. As soon as I starting talking I relaxed. I stood in front of the 30+ students and gave the "me" speech.

I did it without a single "uh" or "um." Immediately after class Mr. Stanforth said he was very impressed, my speech was the best he'd ever heard from a student, and I should consider something to do with speaking as a career. I never gave it a second thought.

Then a few years later in the 9th grade my English class had to do an oral book report. I remember the book I chose to do was *The Lion, The Witch and the Wardrobe*. Today you may know it as a movie based on that section of *The Chronicles of Narnia*. I decided instead of simply doing a report on the book I would be a character in the book. I was the little sister Lucy.

Everyone in my class was dreading giving their report. I was excited. For most people speaking in front of a group, especially one made up of their peers, is their single biggest fear. The second largest fear is death. For some reason I was not afraid or nervous. I was really jazzed up and couldn't wait. The day we were to do our reports, I raised my hand to go first. I couldn't wait to give my little Lucy rendition of *The Lion, The Witch and The Wardrobe*.

I stood up, walked to the podium, and looked at my class. My heart was racing and I felt this charge. I felt a major sense of excitement and exhilaration.

I started my book report. Every eye was on me in complete awe. I was one with the room. I almost had an out of body experience. It seemed as if I was watching me from their eyes. It was a truly profound experience. Fifteen minutes, maybe twenty, went by and I was finishing my report. I had never felt so alive. I was beyond exhilarated. I felt like I was flying and getting the biggest rush of my life.

Of course life has a tendency to get in the way. At this point I had half a dozen experiences where the universe was telling me this is what I was meant to do. Being a teenager in the spotlight, and liking it, meant you were a either a showoff or a loudmouth (not the most favorable labels for a kid). Regardless, whenever a presentation came up in school I looked forward to the opportunity to do better than the last time.

Sophomore year rolled around and again in English class an oral book report was required. Everyone, except me, was dreading it. This time my book was My Fair Lady. To this day it is still my favorite movie and play.

Who was my character? Well, Eliza Doolittle, of course. Once again, I truly loved the experience. Several of my classmates told me that they didn't know how I did it. "You are amazing. When we have to do this, you take the perspective of, "Hey if I have to do it, I may as well rock at it." I remember saying back "If it has to be done I may as well go for it. What have I got to lose?" To this day I have that exact same perspective.

As I mentioned earlier I have no recollection of ever being encouraged by any one of my teachers or counselors, other than Mr. Stanforth the 7th grade school psychologist, to think about public speaking as a career. I do remember having an assembly my sophomore year that was another awakening for me. There was a speaker who came in and was addressing the whole school. There were those big white screens on the stage that showed the speaker as he was talking. There was loud, awesome, motivating music in the background. I was mesmerized. I remember thinking "I wish that were me. I would love to do that. I can see myself doing that."

School went on and I don't remember any more presentations or oral book reports. Somehow I got involved in other things. By the time graduation was near, I found a fondness for manicuring. I went to beauty school, got my license, and started doing nails for a living. Then I moved and got married, started working in a mall doing retail. Then I got divorced, moved six hours away and started doing temp work. Temp work led me to MCI, where I was an administrative assistant, which led me to a mortgage company, which led to sales. In the sales job I was doing little presentations to small groups and getting that charged up feeling again. I was a sales person who made great money and enjoyed it. It never dawned on me to explore a career in speaking.

A few years later, I got a call from my boss who said she was supposed to be on a panel for a convention and wondered if I would be able to fill in for her. I agreed. A week later I was sitting on a panel of four people. There were three men and me.

There were about 100 people in the audience. I gave my five to seven minute speech and took my seat for the Q and A session. Once again I felt elated. Later, I had several of my colleagues and members of the audience say "Wow, Shar. You were by far the best panelist. You are a really good speaker."

Two years later, I was at a huge seminar that my company was putting on for its customers. A broker of mine was there and she pointed out that there were six speakers at this all day event and they were all men. That got me thinking, why were there no women? A few days later I went to our head of marketing and asked. His answer was, "We've been looking for a woman but we just haven't found one that fits yet."

I decided to put together a proposal with my content and said that I would like to be the woman speaker. He said, "Okay, we'll give you a shot at the next seminar. It's in two weeks." I was thrilled. Then I found out that the next seminar was expecting two thousand people. I remember thinking, "Yikes what was I thinking, volunteering for this?" Then I thought, "Hey, what's the worst that can happen? I could fail miserably, fall flat on my face, or worse throw up right there on stage.

HHHmmmm. I decided if any of those happened then I would know that speaking in public was not for me.

As I'm sure you have figured out by now that none of the above happened. However, my heart was racing, my palms were sweating, and I had this incredible urge to use the ladies room. A little nervous tendency I had. Which I can assure you never is a good thing. So I went to the bathroom about a dozen times in an hour. Finally, I said to myself "ENOUGH!" You are not going to the bathroom until this is over. I went outside, took a deep breath and did one last run through of my presentation before I went on.

I was standing in the back of a two thousand person audience. I heard my introduction and my name and I started walking towards the stage. I walked up three stairs, stood on the stage and looked out to the audience. An audience so large, I couldn't see to the back of the room. I was sure everyone could hear my heart beating through my chest. I started to speak. My heart rate slowed down, my shoulders relaxed and I felt like I was doing what I was born to do. I had never felt so alive in my thirty years of life. I remember thinking "Oh my God, this is such a rush. I could do this for the rest of my life." And that was it. I knew what I needed to do.

From that moment on I was doing some type of speaking engagement at least once a month. A year later I quit my job as a sales rep and was speaking for a mortgage training group called *loanofficerschool.com*. I knew speaking was my passion. I loved every last second of it. I had been told many times by many people that I was an inspiration. I knew I had something in me that made me want to help others be, do or have everything they had ever wanted. And, Create Your Fate was born.

Each of us has something that drives us. It's something that we can't explain, but we get an absolute rush over it every time we do it or think about it. What is it for you? Whatever it is that gives you that rush, is passion. When you have passion you will take action. You will know what you said you want, really is what you want when you feel passion and can't wait to take action.

Desire may be another word that works for you. Desire lights your fire. When you know what you desire, it will light a fire in you that no one can put out.

Everyone is passionate about something. Something that feels like it is our calling. What is your purpose in life? What is your calling? Ask a professional athlete, doctor, fireman, teacher, or policeman. Most of the time, they knew since they were children what they wanted to be when they grew up. I remember being in kindergarten and saying I wanted to be a teacher. I do believe that is what I am now. I am a teacher, just not in the conventional sense. I teach people through personal coaching or my books or seminars to live the life they love and love the life they live. I inspire people to find what they want and to go out and get it.

Here is a perfect example. When I was married I had a stepdaughter, whom I love and adore to this day. Her name is Julie Atkins. She called me up one day in November very upset. She had just gotten her children's kindergarten school schedule for the following year. With the half days and holidays and the time they got out of school, she and her husband, Shawn, had no one to watch their two kids. They could put them into day care, but the expense was more than they'd make at work.

She had no idea what to do. She had several ideas but none really made practical or financial sense. So I asked her this question. "Julie, in a perfect world what would you want?" Her answer was a teary "I want to stay home and raise my kids. I don't want them to be raised by school and day care." Of course that was followed by "Yeah, right. How is that going to happen? We have to work and we can't live on one income." So I said, "If staying home truly is what you want, then there is a way to make it happen. We just have to find it."

I suggested she focus on what she really wanted. Forget the how for now, and just visualize staying at home and living comfortably on Shawn's income. We could figure out the details later as there were several months before a decision had to be made.

About a week went by and I got another call. This time she asked about her mortgage. She asked if they could consolidate all their debt and car payments and put it onto the equity line on their home. I had been in the mortgage business for 12 years so I had a little expertise in this area. I grabbed my calculator and crunched a few numbers. It turned out that it was a great idea. They could save about $1000 a month and make all their payments comfortably. She called her Dad and got started on the refinance process.

Now there was a little glitch. Living on just Shawn's income would make things a little tight. There wasn't much room for extras, so I said to Julie, "Just be with it for now. We have found a way for you to stay home with the kids. That was the hard part. There must be a way for you to make a little more money, when the kids are at school. There are thousands of things you can do."

She had been in accounting and payroll for years. I knew she could do the books or payroll for a small mom and pop shop or a bunch of them. She could do a number of home based businesses. I knew if this is what she really wanted then everything would fall into place.

For the next couple of months we both tossed some ideas around. Julie, bless her sweet heart, had thought that delivering the newspaper might be a solution. She even got out of bed at the ungodly hour of 3am to see if it was something she could pull off. She really thought she could do it. Now in my opinion, if we were meant to be awake in the dark, God wouldn't have invented the sun! I told her that the paper route was one idea that could work, but that is just one solution in a universe full of abundance. So just for kicks I suggested she stay open to some other possibilities.

That was something I had learned a long time ago. Generally, people get mixed up in the details more than the outcome. Have you ever heard anyone say "I want to win the lottery?" You probably have, or you may have even said it yourself.

My question is always, "Do you really want to win the lottery or do you just want the money?" The answer is generally, "Hhmmm, well now that you said that, I guess how I get the money isn't really important. It's the million dollars I want." That's a perfect example of getting caught up in the details. I always suggest naming the end goal and leaving the details up to the universe.

So what happened with Julie? You are going to love this. A month or so later the refinance went through. They now have payments that save them over one thousand dollars a month. She isn't leaving her job for 7 months so that gives them time to put some money into savings. Things are definitely looking up.

Then my phone rang. Julie hadn't given her notice at work and she knew she was definitely leaving. This woman has a heart the size of the moon so she felt rather guilty. Giving notice was weighing heavily on her.

It was sometime in March at that point and she went in to speak with her boss. Her boss tapped her gently on the hand and said, "We just love you here. What can we do to make you stay?" Julie explained there wasn't really anything that could be done because of the school schedule with the kids. Her boss said, "Ok, but let's just see if there is something we can work out with on site day care."

Julie had been literally losing sleep at night with the anticipation of having the "I'm quitting" talk. As you will see in the next couple chapters, there are real fears and there are fake fears. Most of the time we make things far worse in our heads than what's real ever turns out to be.

She had given her notice and her boss was trying to make it easier on her. A month or so went by. She went to Julie to say that she bounced a couple of ideas around the rest of the administration and there wasn't anything that could be done about on site day care.

Now you are probably thinking, this is not the way this is supposed to work out. So far things were going really well. Julie had always wanted to be a stay at home mom and now she and her husband were able to make that happen. The only less than perfect thing was money would be tight, but still manageable.

As I mentioned before, the end result is what's important, not getting there. Leave that up to the universe. When Julie had the conversation with her boss, she said, "We love what you've done here and we really don't want to lose you. Why don't you put together a plan where you could do your job or parts of the job part time and from home?"

I'm sure you can imagine Julie was ecstatic to say the least. I got another phone call from Julie that afternoon. This time there were tears of joy in her voice.

She couldn't believe how this had all worked out. Six months ago, she had no idea how she was going to get the kids to and from school, have day care after school and on holidays and on minimum days and still work in order to pay for it all. Today she is going to be a stay at home mom because she wanted to raise her kids, not have daycare do it for her.

They had refinanced their home to make their payments manageable and she can continue working, from home and on a smaller scale for a company that she thoroughly enjoyed working for. Now that seems a whole lot better than a paper route!

Julie called again a couple of days later. She said, "I can't believe how this all worked out. Last November it seemed hopeless. I was lying in bed last night when I realized it was you who asked that one important question. 'Julie, in a perfect world what would you want?' I remember my answer was, "Well I want to be a stay at home mom without having to worry about how to make ends meet.'" She also mentioned after she said that she thought, "Yeah, right. How is that ever going to happen?" Turns out, ask and you shall receive, means a lot more to Julie that it once did.

First thing she needed to do was identify what she really wanted. What was her true desire, her passion? Forget the how. For right now just stick with the idea of what you want. The universe came up with a far better plan for the how. Much better than Julie or I could have ever done.

People generally think there are limitations to what they can have. There are no limits for the universe. I'm sure if you asked Oprah or Donald Trump if there were limits to how much money one can make or things one can do, the answer would be no.

By clarifying what you want, which is "knowin where your goin," and have it be your true desire and your true passion, you can be, do, or have anything. The universe will provide you with the tools. All you have to do is MAP them.

When you have passion you will take action. This is true for anything you have passion for. I had a friend who had a very tough time getting out of bed in the morning. She just wanted to curl up and pull the covers over her head. I'm sure you can relate. That has happened to the best of us. I asked her a simple but important question. "What do you love to do?" She had gotten into running recently and was training for a marathon. It was something that she was completely passionate about. She looked forward to that one hour where she could feel her feet on the pavement. She could clear her head, get her blood pumping, and feel alive. It seemed to be the one thing at that time that made life feel less complicated.

I could see the look in her eyes and hear the excitement in her voice when she spoke about running and what it did for her. At that point I suggested she use her passion to create some action. Run first thing in the morning to get you charged up. And that was it. Every day she got out of bed to do the one thing at that moment that she was completely passionate about. She is who inspired me to write this piece of Create Your Fate. Something so simple like running, or for me it was writing, to get you started on your day.

Doesn't that seem like a great way to get yourself going? With something you love to do. Are you a reader? Then get up a little earlier every day and read. Trust me, waking up won't be a problem, no matter what the hour, when you have something you love waiting for you.

As I mentioned earlier, if God intended for us to be awake in the dark, He would not have created the sun. However, I can honestly say that several days a week I wake up between 3 and 4 in the morning. Sounds hideous, doesn't it? There are days that I just can't wait to write. My best days are those that I begin with the passion for what I was born to do.

When you know what you desire it will light your fire. Ask yourself the important question "What do I really want?" It can be anything you want to be, do, or have. Then write it down and MAP it. Forget everything you hear. When your friends or family tell you that it can't be done, find new friends and spend less time with your family. If someone says it can't be done, what they are really saying is they couldn't or wouldn't do it or they don't want you to because they will feel less about themselves.

Passion equals action. When you find yours, you will create your fate.

Notes: What did I get out of this chapter? What do I want to remember? Etc.

_____

_____

_____

_____

_____

_____

_____

_____

_____

_____

_____

_____

_____

_____

_____

_____

Chapter Four

Lessin Your Stressin

Now is How. Stress. That is probably a word that you hear several times every day. Perhaps you are the one that is feeling stressed. There is a way to eliminate stress from your life. I am going to give you the tools to live in the moment and say goodbye to stress.

Stress is a frame of mind. Now don't close the book and grunt or grumble. After reading this chapter, if you apply what you learn you will not feel stressed ever again. And just in case you do, you will now have a way to release it.

Stress is created by focusing your attention on what happened yesterday or what is coming tomorrow. Or in the bigger picture, dwelling on the past or anticipating the future. Let me ask you this very important question. Is there anything you can do, anything at all, to change something that happened yesterday? You know the answer is no.

The same holds true for tomorrow. Is there anything you can do that will make tomorrow get here any faster? No. Tomorrow will get here when the earth turns on its axis at the speed it always does and completes a full rotation. There isn't anything you can do to rewind or fast forward.

Paying attention to this one second is the only thing you can do. Think about this…

What can happen in a second? Ask a trauma surgeon in a hospital if a second is important. We know for a surgeon or even the patient for that matter, a second can be the difference between life and death.

What about a millisecond? Ask a professional basketball player if a millisecond can be the difference between winning and losing. If the ball is out of a player's hands in the one tenth of a second before the buzzer and the ball goes in the hoop, the shot counts. That's the difference of being the NBA champions or not. Ask a speedskater, or downhill skier in the Olympics if a millisecond can make all the difference in the world. We know it can be the difference between silver and gold.

Now think about a minute. Does a minute have importance? Ask a survivor of the tsunamis in the Indian Ocean on December 26, 2004 if a minute mattered. There would have been many more survivors had they realized what was happening and started running a minute sooner.

How important is an hour? On a lighter note, ask anyone who lives in a high traffic area if getting on the road an hour earlier makes a difference. That hour is huge, especially if you were on your way to your child's school play, softball game or ballet recital. It would just so happen to be the one where he/she made their first home run, or played the lead. And if you had left just an hour earlier you would have seen it.

This takes us to a day. Can a day change your life? I think this one is simple. The best example is 9/11. Did our lives change that day forever? Yes it did. It changed families, friends, national security procedures, and worldwide opinions on terrorism. Everyone's life changed on that day.

Days add up to be a week. How important is a week? Ask a patient with terminal cancer if a week is valuable.

How important is a month? Ask a mother who gave birth prematurely to her child how much value is in a month. That month is the difference between taking her baby home the day after it was born and seeing it in an incubator for several months.

Now is the only thing you have any effect on. Looking to the past or worrying about the future will only keep you from making progress toward what you want. Worry about tomorrow and you'll lose today. Tomorrow doesn't exist anyway. It doesn't get here quicker by losing sleep now. On the flip side, the past doesn't change by focusing your attention on it.

I have a little story that proves how true this is. I was talking to a woman who worked with her husband. They were both clients of mine in the mortgage business. I had worked with them for about a year and found out they had been married for 25 years. Their names are Jo and Kevin Holt. I knew they were married; just not to each other. Anyway, I found out they were married, to each other, on their 25th anniversary.

They both had said that they are happier today than they were when they were initially married. And they were happy then. Jo told me that they had never had a fight. I, as I'm sure you are, was dumbfounded that a couple could go a year much less 25, without a single fight.

First I asked, "Are you serious?" Then I asked, "How have you managed every day for 25 years to not have a fight?" She said, "We decided when we got married anger was not going to fix anything. If we had a problem we would work our way through it, together. Likelihood is whatever we were arguing about doesn't really matter in the big scheme of things and in a year we wouldn't remember it anyway. We realized if either one of us said something in anger, then something bad happened to the other, one of us would have to live the rest of their life knowing the last thing said was less than loving."

"You don't know if what you say to someone will be the last thing you get to say. If anything ever did happen, I want him to have his last moment knowing that I loved him. And if I had to live the rest of my life without him, I want to remember that my last moment with him was a loving one." After hearing that, living in the moment took on a whole new meaning to me.

This couple spent 25 years together. That is 9,125 days. 219,000 hours, 13,140,000 minutes and 788,400,000 seconds, without a single fight. That's over 788 million seconds recognizing the value of each and every one of them. Now that's living in the moment.

The moral of the story is—the absolute best way to have a wonderful life on your own or with someone else is to focus your attention on the one thing you really have. Right now, this moment. Once it's done, you can't undo it. You cannot turn back the clock and change history.

Now I am sure this couple didn't always agree. I'm sure there were things over the years that irritated the other. The bottom line is that harping on something that happened last week or last month or whenever is not going to change what happened. This couple focused on the moment. They didn't build resentment over the past or project into the future. So you can either take action by discussing it before it becomes blown out of proportion or you can accept it and move on to the next moment.

Please don't misread my intentions. I am not saying for you to put your head in the sand and ignore your situation. Do you have rent to pay and no money to pay it? Thinking about it does nothing to get the rent paid.

If you were in a car accident that was your fault, thinking about it and losing sleep over what you should have done differently will not change what happened. You can only make better choices from this point forward. Use this moment to make a difference. If you are short on money, get another job or get a second one. If you were in or caused an accident because you were on the phone then don't drive distracted. If you are upset with your spouse or partner, talk about it now. Not three weeks later when you have had time to fuss and fume and really get riled up.

You can't change other people. Are you married to someone who drives you nuts or perhaps is abusive? It comes down to action or acceptance. Don't complain about something if you are not going to do anything about it. If you are with someone who is hurting you physically or otherwise, you can stay or leave. If you choose to stay you are choosing to accept everything that goes along with staying. Or you can leave, and accept everything that goes along with leaving. Stay and willingly accept or leave and take action.

I remember in a movie I once saw, there was a line that said "closing your eyes to the problem doesn't make it go away." The response was, "neither does talk." Do you continuously talk about things that are wrong in your life? Now for the bigger question, do you do anything about it?

I was dating a man who everyday complained about the same thing regarding his work. He was self-employed and had a couple of employees who were bugging him. Together we came up with several plans, procedures and strategies to rectify the situation.

Two months later he had done none of them. The next time he complained I said, "I'm sorry you are having these issues. However, we came up with several solutions but you're not applying them. You are obviously getting more out of complaining because you could fix the problem but you choose not to. Therefore, I am no longer going to continue to listen. You have two choices, you can act or accept. If you are not going to do what you need to do, then accept it for what it is and stop talking about it." As a wise person once said, "You can curse the darkness or you can strike a match."

I know this sounds harsh but it is completely true. Does talking about something with no action make it be different? No. This applies to so many things in our lives. For years and years I was constantly disappointed in my father. I spent years and thousands of dollars in therapy with hopes of making him be different. One day my therapist said "Shar, you are spending a lot of energy trying to make him be different. When are you going to realize he is who he is and no matter what you do he is not going to be who you want him to be?"

Talk about an epiphany!!! From that moment on I was free from the disappointment of my dad. He is who he is and no amount of dwelling on it will make it be different. So I chose to accept it and move on.

Are you overweight? Do you hate your job? Do you not make enough money? If you think about it, but do nothing about it, it won't change. If you are overweight sitting on your bum eating potato chips won't make you thin. Start to exercise and eat healthy foods. If you don't like your job, talking or thinking about it won't make it be any different. Look for a new one. "Ah," but you say, "if I leave my job then I will lose my retirement and all that I have worked so hard for." Then accept it for what it is. Know that you don't like what you do but keeping your retirement is more important. That's ok. Therefore, acceptance is your answer.

Do you not make enough money? Thinking, or talking, about not making enough money is not going to make you more money. Find a way to make more. Find a job that pays more, take on a second job, go back to school to get educated and trained to do a different one. It comes down to action or acceptance.

There are 86,400 seconds in a day. You can't save up any from yesterday or borrow any from tomorrow. What are you going to do with your 86,400 deposit? I spent years thinking and dwelling on the childhood I had. Many had it worse and many had it better. Bottom line is I can't change it.

Then I realized that without all the bad things that occurred in my life I wouldn't be who I am today. Perhaps all those things happened to make me a stronger person. If you have something in your past that you don't like, find the good in it. Chances are you wouldn't be who you are today without it. If you don't like who you are now, you can be different in the next second. Focus on now and you will make a difference in your life and in the life of others.

Focus your attention on now. That is how you create your fate.

Unwind Your Mind. This is another way for you to lessin your stressin. We think and think and think, but still come up with no solution. Give your mind a rest. It is amazing how many wonderful things happen when you take the time to quiet your thoughts. Give your mind a rest. When you are really upset or worried about something and you simply can not stop thinking about it, this is when you need to quiet your mind the most.

Ever wonder why the best ideas come to you in the middle the night when you are sleeping? That's because your mind is quiet. There are ways to make your mind quiet even when you are not sleeping.

First, let's take a step back to what we just covered. Is thinking about the problem over and over again doing any good? Not likely. At this point, ask yourself this question. Do I want to accept or act? If the answer is acceptance then there really is nothing to be done. If the answer is to act, then you need to find the answer and take action.

Take a moment to sit and be quiet with no thoughts in your head. This will likely seem impossible. If it does, think of something else. Basically, find a distraction. If you have something on your mind think about something else. Read a book, listen to the radio, or call a friend. Do anything to get your mind off of what is bothering you. It's easier said than done, I know. It is a simple solution that is hard to do. But find a way to do it anyway.

Here's a simple silly example that I am sure just about everyone can relate to. Just the other day I was talking to a friend about a movie. It had a line in it: "all relationships end badly otherwise it wouldn't end." Oh, you know the one. The movie with Tom Cruise and what's her name? The blonde from *The Karate Kid*. *Cocktail* is the name of the movie. Honestly, as I write this I cannot for the life of me think of her name. I can see her face and I cannot remember her name. This just happened the other day when I was on the phone with my friend. I know that I know her name. The more I think about it the more I cannot think of her name. Of course now it's just going to bug me.

The more I try to think of her name the more I cannot recall it. I know that is a silly example but the easiest to relate to. Just for kicks, here is another one. I was on vacation with a girlfriend, Tracy, who has restless leg syndrome. We were talking about a new medication that had come out for it and she said it was the same medication that was given to... patients that have the disease where your body shakes or jumps a lot. You know the one. It's the one that Michael J. Fox has.

Oh what is it called? My girlfriend said it started with an A. What is it? Darn it, I know it and I can't think of it. Both of us were stumped and completely annoyed that we couldn't think of it. Neither one of us could think of the darn name. We literally must have spent at least five to ten straight minutes thinking about it. The more we thought the less came to mind. Then we got onto some other subject. Instantly just a few minutes after changing the subject, I said out loud "Parkinson's disease!!!" Tracy said "YES. That's it."

I'm sure you get my point. The more you focus on what you are looking for the less the answers come to you. A simple distraction is enough to open your mind and let the answers come.

This happened to me in the mortgage business all the time. I would get a loan in but it wouldn't fit the guidelines one way or another. I would look through the file over and over and over again and could not find a way to make it work. Eventually, sometimes after hours of working on it, I would set it aside and say "Forget it, I can't figure it out. I'm done." Then I moved on to other things. Of course, shortly after setting it aside the answer would come to me.

Oh, and in case you were wondering, the actress that was in the movie Cocktail with Tom Cruise was Elizabeth Shue. But again, the more I thought about it the more I couldn't think of her name. As soon as I moved onto other things, it popped into my head.

I know an actor's name or the name of a disease is of no importance in the big scheme of things. Or even in the small scheme of things for that matter. But, something so futile and inconsequential and I couldn't think of the answer. Imagine how much harder it is to come up with the right answer when the stakes are really high, when it is something that really matters.

Think about the earlier example with Julie. The more she thought about the solution the less she was able to come up with one. As soon as she was able to get her mind onto something else, refinancing her second mortgage came to mind.

Here is another real life example. I had a friend who was buying her first condo. She had gotten a loan that required a down payment. She had some of it but not all. She really wanted this place but was stuck on how she was going to get the down payment. She was a few thousand dollars short. She called me one day to ask for advice. We thought and thought and couldn't come up with a way to get the money. She was already in contract and if she backed out now she was going to lose her deposit.

I had a similar situation several years earlier. I was buying my first condo and was lacking enough money for the down payment. I had gotten a job at Denny's for a few months on Friday, Saturday and Sunday. I suggested she do the same. She could work on the weekends and save the money she needed. Hhmmm. That just might work.

The next day when I got to work I grabbed my calculator and figured at minimum wage of $4.25 times 8 hours, times 3 days a week (Friday, Saturday and Sunday), times 8 weeks equaled $816. And she would also be making tips. If she made $100 a night in tips, times 3 nights a week, for 8 weeks that would be $2,400. She could claim exempt to could keep the majority of the minimum wage and would have about $3,000 in the next two months, which was exactly what she needed. She had gotten a second job waiting tables somewhere and had a gigantic garage sale. A few months later she moved into her condo.

Was it easy? No. When I did it I was working seven days a week for two months straight. On Sunday, I would work from 11pm to 7am at Denny's, go home, shower and go to my day job from 8 to 5. But, I told myself over and over again, "It's only two months. You can do anything for two months." I made the decision to accept or take action. I wanted the condo and I needed the down payment. I could accept that I didn't have the down payment and not buy the condo, or I could work a second job for a few months, sacrifice a little sleep and buy the condo. I chose to take action and get a second job. So did my friend.

When she had originally called me she had been racking her brain trying to figure out what to do and couldn't come up with anything. Sometimes it is hard to see the forest through the trees. In less metaphorical terms, sometimes it's hard to see the way out of your own mess.

So, what happens if you are in the middle of a mess that you would rather not tell anyone else about? This is when you need to consult a higher power. It could be the universe, God, Spirit, Buddha or whatever you feel comfortable with. Basically, pray or meditate. Take a few minutes to quiet your mind and let the answer come to you. If nothing jumps in your mind right away, just accept that you are stumped for the moment. Just know that there is an answer, you just don't know what it is yet.

The first thing to do is meditate. The second thing is identifying the end result. What is it that you want? You don't have to know how you are going to get it, but at least tell the universe what you want. Imagine you have what you want and feel how it would feel as if it existed right now. Then, go on about your day. Find a good distraction. Read a book, go to a movie, play some golf, go for a workout and listen to some music. Do anything to take your mind off of the problem.

A lot of people would say "Isn't that just being in denial?" No it isn't. It's accepting the fact that you have a problem and you don't have a solution. The more you think about the solution the more stumped you get. Just like when I was trying to remember Elizabeth Shue's name. The harder I thought about it, the less the answer came to me.

Focus your attention on what you want and you will get it. Focus your attention on what you don't want and you'll get it, too. Therefore, quiet your mind, think about what you want as an end result, imagine what it would feel like to have it, go on about your day, and let the universe give you the answers.

And that is how to lessin your stressin.

Notes: What did I get out of this chapter? What do I want to remember? Etc.

_____

_____

_____

_____

_____

_____

_____

_____

_____

_____

_____

_____

_____

_____

_____

_____

Chapter Five

Farewell to Fear

Fear. It stops us in our tracks like nothing else. However, the truth is most things we fear don't even exist.

I'm not talking about snakes or black widow spiders. I'm talking about the fears that keep us from reaching our goal or sometimes stop us from ever trying for them. There are real fears, and there are fake ones.

If you were swimming in the ocean and were surrounded by a bunch of sharks that could eat you, you'd have every right to be afraid. That would be a real fear. Let's say you are allergic to bees and are surrounded by a swarm of them. Again, it is completely reasonable to be afraid.

These are real fears. Real fears are things that can literally cause you physical harm or death. Fake fears are things that we imagine, but they don't really exist. For instance, the fear of rejection would be a fake fear. It doesn't really exist, right? It is the idea of being rejected that scares you. It is what could happen that stops you in your tracks. But would rejection cause you physical harm or death? No. Again, it is a fear that is based on something that doesn't exist.

Here is a fabulous example. I was traveling from San Francisco to Orange County. A girlfriend and I were sitting in a restaurant waiting for our flight to board. I saw a very attractive man a few tables away. I pointed him out to my girlfriend and said I was going to go up to him say hello and give him my card. She looked at me and said out loud, "Are you crazy? What if he says, 'get lost loser?'"

To make a long story short I did nothing at that moment. However, he was at the same gate, on the same plane, going to the same place. When we arrived in Orange County we were waiting for our luggage and there he was again, standing at baggage claim. I told my girlfriend I'd be right back. I grabbed my card walked straight up to him and said these exact words. "Hi, my name is Sharmen Lane and I noticed you in the restaurant in San Francisco. You look like someone I would like to get to know better. If you are from here, single and interested, call me." I handed him my card at which point he held out his hand and gave me his name. I shook his hand and said, "Nice to meet you, hope to talk to you soon," and I walked away.

I walked back to my friend whose chin was on the floor. All she could say was, "You are so rad!" She said she couldn't believe I had done that. These were my exact words back. "Serene, I figured there were a few things that could happen. A. He says, 'get lost.' B. He calls. C. He doesn't call. D. He calls, we go out, and there's no chemistry and I never see him again. Or, E. He calls, we hit it off, we get married, have kids and in ten years when our kids ask, "How did you and daddy meet?' I can say, 'I saw him in an airport and just had to have him.'"

What a story, huh? Just so you know, the latter did not happen. He called and we set up a date, but he had to cancel. We rescheduled, then I cancelled; then he cancelled and we never did get together. The point here is this. I could have done nothing and always wondered what would have happened if. Now I don't have to wonder. I tried, it didn't work out, I moved on. In my opinion, there was no losing. You regret the things you don't do and learn from the things you do.

I have learned to not take anything personally. He could have been a real jerk and said, "Who do you think you are talking to a stud like me?" If he did, it would have said more about him than it did about me and I would know that he was not anywhere close to the man I wanted to be with. Again, there was no bad news. If he did "reject me", then it was his loss and he missed out on the best thing that could have ever happened to him. It's like Wayne Gretzky said. You miss one hundred percent of the shots you don't take. I would rather take a shot, miss, and know that I tried than to wonder what would have happened "If."

In my mind there was really nothing to lose. I was a little nervous when I walked up to him but I had a quick conversation with myself. It went something like this. "Shar, what's bigger you or your fear? If he says 'get lost' will it physically cause you harm or will you die? Nope. Then what are you waiting for? Go talk to him."

I actually had a coaching client that was dreadfully afraid of going into real estate agents offices. She had a tremendous fear of rejection. I asked her what the problem was. "Why are you so afraid to go into these offices?" Her response was, and I'm paraphrasing, "I just can't. My parents were divorced when I was two, I didn't see my Dad much, my mother always told me I wouldn't amount to anything. So I pretty much felt rejected by both my parents and that has been something I have dealt with my entire life."

That's pretty powerful stuff. I certainly understood and empathized. However, I asked her if she physically couldn't walk to the door, extend her arm, open the door and walk in? Naturally, her answer was, "Well, yes I could do that." I let her know that there is a big difference between "can't" and "won't." "Can't" means, "it is not physically possible." "Won't" means, "You are physically capable but choose not to." After considering this for a moment, she reluctantly agreed.

I then asked if there was any bodily harm that could occur from her walking in and talking to real estate agents. Of course the answer was no. Then I asked, "Is there any possibility that you could die from talking to them?" Again, the answer was, "No" "So," I asked, "what is the worst thing that could happen?" She said, "They could tell me to get out of their office and not waste their time." I said, "Is that all?" Her answer was "Yes."

In a nutshell, I said, let me get this straight. You won't be physically hurt. You won't die. However, you are inhibiting your success because someone could be rude and tell you to get out of their office? Sheepishly, she said, "Yes I suppose that is what I'm saying." Then I said, "By the way, if someone were to say that, the person is likely a jerk to everyone and it simply says that he or she is a miserably unhappy individual and wants everyone he comes in contact with to be just as miserable as he is. It has nothing to do with you." "You're right", she finally said.

Then I told her over the next week she was to go into five real estate broker offices. I also let her know that there was no excuse that would be acceptable for her not doing this. I gave her this last example. Think about when you were a child and you thought the wrinkles in your bed were snakes or there was a monster on the wall. You turned on a light and saw that there were no snakes or monsters. There were just wrinkles and shadows. That is what we have done today. We have turned on the light to see what is real. Now the things that were fake, no longer exist. From that moment on this woman said farewell to fear, took charge of her life, and did more than she ever thought possible.

I suggested that every time something came up that was holding her back, she ask herself the question, "Is this a real fear, or a fake fear? Could this cause me physical harm or death?" Most of what we fear only exists in our heads. It's just our imagination. Once you realize that, you will know that anything is possible and the only thing holding you back is you.

There are many fake fears. I am not diminishing their existence. I am however diminishing their power. Fear of failure, fear of loss, fear of abandonment, fear of rejection. The list goes on and on. However, they are all things that don't exist. They are a projection into the future of what might happen or what could potentially happen.

In my mind I am not going to be held hostage by something that cannot cause physical harm or death and really only exists in my head.

Perception is reality. Even if I did fail at something, did I learn from it? If I learned something then I really didn't fail. I didn't lose anything. I simply gained new knowledge and information. I learned that what I did, didn't work. So, I either can take action by finding a different way to do it. Or I can accept that it wasn't my thing and move on to something that is.

When you say farewell to fear, you say hello to happiness.

Notes: What did I get out of this chapter? What do I want to remember? Etc.

_____

_____

_____

_____

_____

_____

_____

_____

_____

_____

_____

_____

_____

_____

_____

_____

_____

Chapter Six

What You Believe Is What You'll Receive

What came first the chicken or the egg? Did the egg hatch and out came the chicken, or did the chicken lay the egg that later hatched? If the chicken is required to produce the egg, but the egg is what produces the chicken, which came first? Good question and quite the conundrum.

The things you have in your life, did you believe before you received? Did you receive then believe? I'm sure you've said or heard this before…I'll believe it when I see it. If you see it in your mind first, you will receive it. It's all in your head.

All things begin with a thought or idea. Think about all of the wonderful modern conveniences we have in our world today. Computers, televisions, jet engine airplanes—the list goes on and on. Someone had to have the vision of these things first. Then they had to believe they were possible. Believed then received. The thought or idea began in someone's mind then they put it into motion.

You must first create what you want in your head. Let it exist there first. Then allow it to expand and to come to fruition. This happens to all of us every day. You were thinking of a person and the next thing you know he or she calls. You hear of a movie that day and there it is on TV that night. You were just looking for something and the next day there's an ad in the paper for it. The vision comes to fruition.

Years ago I wanted to be a phlebotomist. I had a friend who worked in the admission's department of a hospital. She gave me the name of the supervisor of the lab department. When I spoke to him he said they didn't train, and to get hired you had to be experienced. So I asked where to get training. He said he didn't know. I asked other hospitals and lab technicians and everyone seemed to have been working at the hospital first, doing something else, and somehow got training later for phlebotomy.

This was before the Internet existed so I couldn't simply Google it. After a couple weeks of searching I said out loud. "Universe, I've done all I can. I believe it's out there, you show me where to find it." I clearly remember three days later I was in line at a department store and the lady in front of me said something about getting her phlebotomy certification. My ears perked up and I asked her where she got her training. She said that a man at the hospital she worked at gave a little weekend training course. I asked her which hospital she worked at, which city it was in, and what this persons name was. She gave me the information and I called the next day. The man said the name of his little training center was called The Phlebotomy Group and to call his office to get details for the next class. First I had to believe the answer was out there, then I received exactly what I was looking for.

Do you believe that you deserve the very best that the world has to offer? I don't want to be rich; I just want to be comfortable. Ever heard that one before? Why not be rich? I have a friend that says she feels guilty asking for anything more. She has a nice house, good job, good income. "Who am I to ask for more, when I have so much already?" I said, "Just because you have more doesn't mean you are taking it from someone else." Actually it is just the opposite. The more money you have, the more you'll spend. The more you spend is the more a store will make. Someone owns the store so they will make more. The salesperson who works there will make more commission, which means he will spend more. Which means someone else will make more from his spending more and so on and so on.

Better yet, the more money you make the more you will give away. You think you have enough and don't want to take from others who have less. How about making more just because you can, so that you can donate to charity. Give something to those who have less. That is truly a better plan than simply not asking for more because you feel guilty. If you don't believe you should have more then you won't. Maybe you need to rationalize in your own head why you deserve more. The more I have, the more I give away. Now you believe there is a reason you should have more and the next thing you know you will receive more.

There are many different levels of receiving. With my personal coaching program I get people who are having a tough time in a bunch of different areas. Some have trouble finding the person they want to be in a relationship with. Others can't seem to make enough money, or find the right job. Most are having a hard time partly because they don't really know what they are looking for. So this is step one, knowin where you're goin, or identifying exactly what you want.

A few years ago I traveled with a friend who had recently split up with her boyfriend. During the flight I had suggested that we write out her dream man list. You may be thinking, "What's a dream man list?" So was she. I said, "It's really important to write down the things you know you want your partner to have. Otherwise the universe just keeps on throwing stuff at you until it gets it right."

So I grabbed a piece of paper and told her to randomly throw out thoughts and ideas of what she wanted the man of her dreams to be like. Then I asked the all important question. Do you believe someone like this exists? After a moment of thinking she said, "Yes, I do." Then I said, "Picture him in your mind. Not just how he looks but how it would feel to have him." Do you believe you can have that? Once again she said "yes."

Less than 30 days later a man with everything on her list, and I do mean everything, walked into her life. She later realized there were some things she wanted but didn't think about when we were writing her list.

She realized those things were pretty important to her and, unfortunately, this man didn't have them. They ended up breaking up about a year later and she did another dream man list. This time around she was sure to add those things that were missing to her list. It took a little bit longer this time but dream man from list number two showed up. They have been happily together for a few years now.

I have done this with dozens and dozens of people and just like this friend within a very, very short time, generally days to a few of weeks at most, the dream man or woman showed up in their life. Being specific is very important. As the previous example showed, this woman had forgotten to mention a couple of things on her list that were extremely important. The same thing happened to me. I was in my early twenties and wrote out my dream man list. An item of mine was that he be, and this is exactly what I wrote, at least 28. Literally less than a month later he appeared. One minor detail, he was exactly 28 years OLDER than I. I guess I needed to be more specific.

Please don't let anyone tell you what to believe. That is completely up to you to decide. I have friends, family, colleagues, etc, who tell me I'm too picky about the man I want as a partner. I don't care if you are talking about your dream spouse, job, career, home, car or whatever. You can have exactly what you want. If you believe, you will receive. What you believe is entirely up to you.

Use the visual map idea that I mentioned in chapter 2. Cut out pictures of what you want and put yourself in them. I put a picture of my face on the cover of Time magazine, Oprah magazine, on the back of book covers with my name all over it. I was so sure of what I wanted that I put it in front of me every day so I would be reminded of what I wanted and the things I needed to do to get it.

I also started spending more time alone or with a very small group of people. I didn't want to be around anyone who didn't believe in me or my passion. I would only spend time with people that I wanted be like or with close friends that believed in me and my goal. If you want to know what you will be like in 6 months to a year, look around you. The people you spend your time with are likely who you are going to become. Most of us default to the lowest common denominator. It is up to you to believe in something different and raise yourself and those around you to a higher level.

Have you ever heard of Synergy? Synergy is defined as: The interaction of two or more agents or forces so that their combined effect is greater than the sum of their individual effects. In more simple terms the sum of the whole is greater than its parts. What does this mean and how can you make it work for you?

You're conscious mind is a powerful thing. It is aware of everything at every moment. Your subconscious mind is extraordinarily powerful. It is aware of everything that goes on behind the scenes that you aren't fully cognizant of. Most of us know that things can be buried so deep in our subconscious mind that we have no idea they ever existed in the first place. Everything we have seen, touched, tasted, felt is all stored in this hard drive in our mind. Your eyes see everything whether you are aware of it or not.

Your conscious mind is aware of everything you are giving your full attention to. Making your conscious and subconscious mind work together will help you achieve anything. How do you make them both work together to synergize?

Your subconscious mind does not know the difference between what is real and what is fake. Think about your dreams. Better yet, think about a nightmare. You are sleeping and have a picture in your mind of a man chasing you on a rooftop. He reaches you puts his hand around your throat and is choking you. You're struggling trying to break away. You're dangerously close to the edge. You lose your footing and fall over the edge. You are falling and just before you hit the ground your body jumps and you wake up. What is happening to your body? Are you sweating, breathing heavy, is your heart racing? Your body is responding to a message that your subconscious mind had, but wasn't real.

You might be thinking, "That's great, but how does that help me?" If you heard something over and over and over again, and it was something that you had an emotion about, you would believe it regardless of whether or not it was true. That is repetition and emotion. Using those two things in a positive way will create synergy. In other words, when you use a conscious tool and associate it with a powerful emotion over and over again you will believe what the tool represented.

A silly but true example, I once did this with a candy bar a couple years ago. I had read something similar and wanted to test it out. I looked at and smelled the candy bar while eating a raw oyster from the shell. Now, if you like oysters this wouldn't be a problem for you. I, however, do not. The bottom line is: I threw up. After smelling the candy bar and eating the oyster, I literally barfed all over the kitchen floor. To this day I cannot look at this particular candy bar without gagging.

How can you use synergy to help you reach your goal? Here's what you do. Take a colored dot. Red, green, yellow, purple, or any color you want. You know what I mean, those little half inch color coding dots available at office supply stores. Choose the color of dot you want. Put it on a piece of paper and I write the words I AM next to it. Now think about your goal. What do you want? Make sure you list it in the present time as if it already exists and state it in the positive. You can say, "I am a multi millionaire. I am a 5'3" 110 pound svelte woman. I am a professional, successful, six figure a year VP." I have a coaching client named Philip who recently wrote his I AM statement, and it's a good one. He wrote, "I AM a business owner on the Forbes list." Now that is a powerful I AM statement. He's not there yet, but he is on his way. The one I have used for the last 6 months is, "I am a seven figure published author and speaker." When I wrote mine I was not published at all. Three months after writing that I AM statement my first book, "Why Am I Special" for preschool age children was published.

I have red dots everywhere my eyes look. They are in my kitchen, living room, bathroom, car, etc. There are literally dozens of little red dots all over the place. I have them on the doorknob, my computer, microwave, refrigerator, lamp, hairdryer, wallet, cell phone, home phone, and rear view mirror. That's just to name a few.

Being a professional speaker and published author is my life's goal. So it's safe to say I am emotionally connected to it. All day every day my eyes are seeing the red dots. For awhile I saw them and said I am a seven figure published author and speaker. Over time I forgot they were there. Friends and family would come to my house and ask "what's with all the red dots?" I told them and nine times out of ten the next time I went to their house they have something similar around as well. Every time I see a red dot my subconscious mind makes a connection. Every time my eyes see a dot it is repeating its meaning. Repetition and emotion. And that is synergy.

You may not realize that other people have done this for you. Most associate with it in a negative way. Has someone said something to you that repeatedly hurt your feelings? Do you carry it with you every day? A couple of my coaching clients said that as children they were told early and often they were stupid and wouldn't amount to anything.

I had one client who was in the mortgage business and had been to my Loan Officer class and several other trainings as well. He really knew his stuff. I had complete confidence that he was ready and could do loans with no problem.

After a couple sessions with him I noticed he wasn't marketing to borrowers. I asked him why. He said "Shar, I'm scared to death." I asked why and he explained the negative messages he got for years and years as a kid. We wrote out a couple of affirmations and I told him to choose the one that really resonated with him. I gave him a bunch of dots and told him to write the affirmation next to it. I said I wanted him to place those dots all over where he would constantly see them and for the next week I wanted him to say the affirmation out loud every time he saw it. I also told him to look in the mirror and say it out loud 10 times first thing in the morning and last thing before he went to bed.

The very next week he had three loans on his desk. Each one was doable and he had never felt so strong and confident in his entire life. He said that he was a changed man and from that moment on he was in charge of the messages that were going to stick in his mind. And that is the power of synergy.

Recently I had a man come to me who was at his wits end. His name is Alan. Alan was in an unhappy relationship, wasn't working, had no money, and had no idea how he was going to pay his next month's rent on his closet sized studio apartment. He told me he was either in tears or darn near every day for the last month.

At that moment I decided to give him the chapters of this book that were complete. I told him to read it with an open heart and open mind. Then I asked him to call me when he was finished and tell me if it had any impact on him.

I didn't hear from him for a few days. Then he called me in tears saying that what he had just read changed his life. He wrote down what he wanted, MAP'd it, and diced it into small doable daily bite size pieces. A week later he'd gone on several interviews and landed a job. It wasn't the job of his dreams, but it was a step in the right direction. By the way, when he wrote out his goals (so he'd be knowin where he was goin), he wrote "I want a job that I can make decent money at to pay my bills." At the time he thought that was all he could get.

A little more time passed and I sent him the next chapter, Passion Equals Action. He emailed me to let me know that he had a terrible day so at his lunch break he printed the latest chapter, went outside and read it. He said he felt overwhelmed by what I had written. Before he read that chapter he had never really thought about what he was passionate about. But now he remembered. He loved boats. His exact words were,

"I love boats. I love to sail them, fix them, build them, etc. They are what I am truly passionate about and the only thing I am good at."

We spoke on the phone later that day and he explained how he got into boating and why he stopped. Like most of us he took something someone said and believed it. A guy at a boat shop who was in charge of financing said some ridiculously condescending remark about him not having what it takes to buy a boat or run one, and he should find something else to do with his life. Unfortunately he took it to heart and walked away leaving his boat dream in the shop behind him. Fifteen years later, he still carried that person's comment around with him—comments from a man whose name he no longer remembered. He couldn't pick him out of a lineup or off the side of a milk carton, but he clearly remembered the words that were said.

The next time you think about saying something derogatory or negative to someone, think about the impact you could have on that person's life. Alan did not know this man, but his words had affected his life dramatically. Imagine parents who tell their children they won't amount to anything, or that they are nothing or that they are worthless. Your path in life could change if someone you don't even know were to say something hurtful. Think about how much worse it would be coming from someone who says they love you. If you are going to affect someone's life wouldn't it be so much better to do it in a good way? Your candle doesn't shine brighter when you blow out someone else's.

Back to Alan. He was telling me why he had gotten out of boating but after reading the chapters I had sent him, he felt that he could be, do or have anything he wanted. Then he said this "Shar, please finish this book. The world needs this. You have such a positive and profound impact on people. You empower others to follow their dream and conquer the world. Please finish this book." He said that he was getting back into boating. He wanted to buy a boat and find a way to make money at it.

Days later Alan called me with the excitement of a little boy who got his first puppy. He told me that he was carrying the chapters he had read in his pocket and was walking his dog at the dock of a marina near his apartment. A boat caught his attention. It caught his attention because it was the same type a friend of his had. He was walking around it thinking of how much work had been done to it because it was an older boat that looked great. Then he saw the "for sale" sign. Of course his first thought was, "I'm broke how can I buy this boat?" Then he tapped his pocket that had pages of my book in it and decided to call the number.

He expressed his interest in the boat and asked if he could take a look at the inside. The owner came and met him. Alan explained his history with boats and said that he wanted to buy it. He explained that he had no money. This man had already turned down several offers because boat people want to know that whoever is buying the boat is going to love and care for it. This man sensed how much Alan loved boats and knew he would take good care of it. They worked out an arrangement so he could pay for it over the next couple months in a few installments. The owner took down the "for sale" signs and shook Alan's hand.

Alan spent the next several nights sitting on that boat looking out at the stars knowing anything is possible if you follow your passion and believe. Before he found this boat his ex-girlfriend told him that she had a friend who was giving away a boat and wanted to know if he wanted it. Also, he had contacted several people who had placed ads in the paper about boat sales and financing. He had looked at almost 30 boats but none felt right. When Alan found the right boat the right opportunity came along with it.

Wouldn't it be great if the story ended there? I think it would. But there's more. A week and a half later Alan called me on Sunday of July 4th weekend. He said, "Shar, you are not going to believe this. I'm at the beach with a friend and ran into an old friend that I haven't seen in years. He owns a yacht shop and surveying business. He just sold the business and is looking for someone to take over the surveying service." As you can imagine Alan was indescribably ecstatic. "This is all because of you and your book. All I did was list what I wanted but had no idea how I was going to get it. Then I remembered the story about Julie and how she just named what she wanted and the universe took care of the rest. Thank you for giving me this gift. Because of you I am getting exactly what I wanted."

A month before Alan couldn't imagine that he would have a boat. Just like Julie, all he had to do was identify what he really wanted and was passionate about. No matter how hard either of them tried, they couldn't come up with a solution that fit. They knew what they wanted and when they released the "how," it all fell into place.

Everything you want is at your fingertips, but you first have to believe it is possible. Your family, friends, boss, or co-workers may think you are out of your mind. So what? I'm sure people said that about DaVinci, Michelangelo, Gandhi, Einstein, Edison, Franklin, etc. etc. etc. I've been criticized for leaving a well paying job to do what I love. Family, friends and perfect strangers have thought I was out of mind. Several still do. It doesn't matter what others say or think. This is your life. Are you going to let anyone else tell you what you deserve? Are you going to let some naysayer dictate your life?

Does the name Erik Weihenmayer sound familiar? This man went blind when he was thirteen due to a genetic eye disease he was born with. He has been on many talk shows for his tremendous accomplishment. He was the first blind man to climb Mount Everest. Climbing Everest is an extraordinary feat for any human being. It's beyond extraordinary for a blind person. He had a goal (knowin where you're goin), put together a plan (MAPing), found his passion and acted on it (passion equals action), rose above his fear (farewell to fear), believed in himself and climbed to the top of the world's highest peak (what you believe is what you'll receive).

Chances are whatever it is that you want to be, do, or have, does not entail blindness and climbing a 29,035 foot mountain. If Erik Weihenmayer climbed Everest, you can do anything you want.

If you say farewell to fear, let passion equal action, you will create your fate. It's all in what you believe.

Notes: What did I get out of this chapter? What do I want to remember? Etc.

_____

_____

_____

_____

_____

_____

_____

_____

_____

_____

_____

_____

_____

_____

_____

_____

_____

Chapter Seven

Manifest Your Best

All the best things in life are just waiting for you. By now you have discovered where you want to go. Then you MAP'd it by coming up with a step by step plan to get it. You diced those steps to come up with daily baby steps to accomplish each of the bigger tasks. You asked yourself that all powerful question "Is this my passion?" because it takes passion to equal action. Along the way, stress and fear may creep up on you. But now you know how to lessin your stressing and say farewell to fear. Lastly, you know all things good, bad, or indifferent first began as a vision in your head and what you believe is what you'll receive. Now you have a toolbox full of utensils to get what you want. But you're not done yet. You have built the ladder to climb up to your goal. Here is the last rung to get you over the top.

There is a little magic trick you can pull out of your hat to ensure your success. It is called the 3 C's to Succcess.

These C's will lock in your goal and waterproof it to make sure you get what you want.

The first C is Commit. Commitment is the toughest of the 3 C's. This is where you figure out if what say you want really is what you want. Let's use the losing weight example again. You decide you want to be healthier, thinner, and leaner. Now it is time to come up with a plan and commit to it. You sign up at a gym. Which requires what? It requires you to sign a contract. Even if you don't use it you are still going to pay for it until your contract ends. You talk to a trainer because you are serious and want to do this right. They tell you all that is involved. The foods you need to eat, the weight training and cardiovascular exercise you will need to do and how often. They tell you how many calories you will be allowed to take in and how many you will need to burn to get to where you want to be.

Two things can happen. Option One. You step up and commit. What happens if you decide later you don't want to work out with the trainer anymore? That's ok, but you signed a contract and paid for your sessions and you are not going to get a refund. Option two. You say, "Ya know what? I don't want to do all this. I had no idea this is what it was going to take and I really don't want it that badly." If you say yes I want to do this then you sign on the dotted line. If you say no, you accept things the way they are and find a way to live with what you have until you are ready to do what is necessary to commit.

Let's say you want to buy a house. There are a lot of things involved and a lot of commitment. Once you find the house you want, you put in an offer. Which is what? It's a contract, a written commitment. Once you sign, you can't simply come back a week later and say "nah, never mind I don't want it anymore." Well, you could, just not without consequences. If you did there could be some financial obligations for backing out after signing.

How about marriage? So many people go into it without really being committed to it for life. I know a lot of people who go into marriage thinking they can get out. Look at the divorce rate and you'll know that's true. There would either be fewer marriages to begin with or fewer divorces if people looked at it as a lifetime commitment. I've done this with my life. I decided that if I were to get married again I would look at it as a lifetime commitment that I can not get out of for any reason. Did you or did someone you know think when they got married that there was no out and this was for life and you can't get out no matter what? I doubt it.

Here is a perfect example from another client of mine. He was divorced and gave the reason that there were things he didn't know about before he got married. He said if he had known ahead of time, he wouldn't have gotten married. Here's what I said. "Ok, let's look at this from an open and honest perspective. You are saying that you had no idea, no sign, no clue that this issue existed?" He responded with "NO. I had no idea." I said "none whatsoever?" He said "Well, I guess I had a little clue, but I thought things would change after we got married." "Alright! That's an honest answer and I respect that."

We continued to talk but here's the gist. I said we generally do have some sign or gut feeling that we really don't want to live with this one thing for the rest of our life. But we delude ourselves into thinking it will be ok or it will change or it will be different when we get married. Here's the problem. What you see is what you have and will continue to get. But we love this person and want to spend our lives with them and there are so many other good things. We say this one thing doesn't really matter. If that "thing" doesn't really matter, then fine. However, usually it does.

What you should do from this point forward is ask yourself "if this 'thing' were to remain as it is and will always be that way, am I willing to live with it forever?" Sometimes the answer will be yes. Sometimes it won't.

Wouldn't you rather not get married knowing this "thing" is a deal breaker than spend the next however many years trying to change the person, resenting them and later divorcing? At which point you have hurt feelings, lost time, wasted energy, spent money and possibly have your children suffer as well.

We generally do know or have a hint of what we are getting ourselves into. BUT, we close our eyes to the things we don't like and think the situation, or the person will change "after we get married." Somehow we are shocked that it didn't and now we want out. If we would think of what we are getting into as a lifetime commitment the divorce rate would go down.

This exact situation happened to me. Before I got married there were a couple things that would not work for me and were deal breakers. He said they'd change after we got married. Shockingly they didn't. I remembered thinking I knew this existed and I should have decided if I was ok with it the way it was and not expected it to change or I shouldn't have gotten married. Hindsight is 20/20. Getting a divorce was the hardest decision I ever made. I can assure you I learned a valuable lesson and make better decisions now because of it.

The person you are going to marry, is he or she a drinker? Does he/she smoke, have a temper, bad with money, messy, disorganized, abusive, bad in bed? Are you willing to live with any or all these things? If it exists now, you aren't going to change it or them. So you need to think thoroughly about what you are getting yourself into. You can't change other people. If a person wants to be different, it is up to them to change. Then they have to take the steps necessary to actually change. But you can't do it for them.

When you buy a car you can't drive it off the lot and change your mind. No buyer's remorse. Anytime you sign a contract you are making a commitment. Whatever you are doing, whatever choice you have to make, view it as a commitment and you will make better decisions and come out better in the end because you did.

Do you want to lose weight? Are you considering a new job or promotion? Are you buying a car or entering into a legal contract? No matter what you are considering, first think about what is real or what is required. Then decide if you want it. And that means you want ALL of it.

The second C to success is communication. The more you communicate your goal to yourself and to others the more likely you are to achieve it. Again, let's use the "losing weight" example. First off the way you communicate with yourself is very important. The words you choose to use when you set goals is very important to your success. I do not use the term "losing weight" because anytime you view something as a loss there is likely going to be some mental or emotional resistance. So choose a goal that is stated in the positive. For example if your ultimate goal is "losing weight", change it to something like, "I want more lean muscle mass, get slimmer, get healthy, strengthen my heart, extend my life, etc." Can you see the difference?

It is so much better to add something rather than take something away. People usually think of dieting or weight loss as painful because they have to give up the foods they like or things they like to do. However, if you put it into the perspective of what you are gaining then you are already more likely to succeed. Instead of saying "I am giving up sugary or fatty foods," say, "I am only eating foods that are good for me. I'm only eating foods that are nutritionally sound."

Remember when you were a child and had something taken away from you for punishment? Didn't you want it even more? That is likely true in your adult life as well. If your doctor says you can't have red meat don't you instantly start to crave a nice big juicy steak? Mostly we want what we can't have. If you view the process of achieving your goal as a plus instead of a minus, you will enjoy the process and get what you want.

The way you communicate to yourself is extremely important but communicating to others is just as important and maybe even more so. Just think, if my goal is to get to my happy weight I am much more likely to accomplish it if I tell everyone around me what my goal is. Tell your family, friends and co-workers what you are working toward. Let's say you are 200 pounds and want to get to 175 or 150 or 120 etc. Tell everyone you work with that you are going to weigh 175 pounds by Christmas. Better yet, put up a sign in your cubical or office. You are a whole lot less likely to hit the Krispy Kreme's in the break room on Fridays if everyone around you knows what you are working towards. This way you will be surrounded by reminders that will keep you on track.

I love to do this. I have my goal written on post it notes and have them all over my home. People come over and ask what's with all the post its. Then I can to share with them what I am working towards. I am not only telling them but I am also repeating it to myself. It is also a proven fact that you will remember something better if you use all your senses to learn it. So if I am telling others then I am using my voice and I am hearing it so I am using my auditory sense as well. Then

I write it down so I am using my hands, which is the tactile sense and then I read it, which is using my visual sense. Then I envision myself being or having whatever it is that I am working towards while imagining what it would feel like to have it. That is using my feelings, and, as a result utilizing my kinesthetic sense.

Hopefully now you see the importance of communication as the second C to success. You must tell everyone around you as well as yourself about your goal. I did this with the book you are reading. For years and years I didn't tell anyone about the book I planned to write. I was teaching a class that had generally 50+ people in it. So at every class I started to share my goal. I had 50+ people every weekend who knew what I was working toward. Then I got emails and phone calls all the time about how it is going. Boy, did that keep me on track! How big of a schmuck did I look like if every time someone asked me how the book was coming and I said "what book? Or "uh yeah, it's on the back burner." I wouldn't have any credibility if I told people what to do and didn't do it myself.

Same thing goes with the dieting example. Let's say, for example, 175 pounds is your goal weight. You've told everyone you know what you goal is. It's posted at your desk and is the screen saver on your computer. Then, on Friday morning, when donuts are in the breakroom, everyone asks "How are you doing on the 175 pound goal?" I really don't think you are going to pop one of the Krispy Kremes into your mouth and say "GREAT!" Even if you were tempted to have one, you are likely a lot less inclined to now. The more people you tell the more people who are there to keep you honest. You know darn good and well that you won't tell everyone you know you are on a mission to fit into the jeans you wore in high school but eat chocolate chips cookies as you say it.

Now let's say you don't share your goal with anyone. Why would you not tell anyone what your goal is? Chances are you don't want anyone to notice when you don't reach it. Isn't that already setting yourself up for failure? I think so. If no one knows that you want to be 175 pounds by Christmas or to fit into those size 8 jeans, then there's no harm in eating that 600 calorie donut with zero nutrition, because no one knew you weren't supposed to have it in the first place. But when there's a witness or two or three or more, you think before you do. You have others to hold you accountable.

This is why a workout buddy or something or someone to keep you honest and on track is a tremendous benefit. That is why people who go to Weight Watchers or Jenny Craig's or have a trainer or a personal coach have higher success rates. There is always someone to answer to. Keeping your goal a secret is a well devised plan for failure and nothing else.

Hundreds of thousands of people lost weight, or, in better terms, gained health, when they were on a program. But then they reach their goal and what do they do? They stop going to meetings or talking to their coach, right? Again, using the weight loss example, what almost always happens??? You gain the weight back. You stopped doing what worked. You stopped having someone or a group of people keep you account-able. You have no one to answer to.

I learned this lesson very quickly when I had my first personal coach. Every time I'd set some objectives for my next week, I felt like a complete nincompoop when I didn't do them. And, boy, did she let me know how much I was degrading my own value or lessening my integrity anytime I failed to follow through on my weekly tasks. If I hadn't told her or anyone else what my intentions were, no one except for me would know I didn't do it. Chances are I'd "forget" what it was I was going to do in the first place. It's kind of like New Year's resolutions. You make a goal and write it down, only it's in some obscure place where no one (includ-ing you by the way) can see it. Then you stumble on it months later to realize you haven't come close to achiev-ing it. If you are serious about accomplishing anything, I suggest you get talking, but don't stop there. Talk, write, read, hear, see, and feel your goal.

Here's one more reason the second C, communi-cate, is important. Have you ever had a flaky friend or someone who was always saying they were going to do something...and never do it? Better yet. Has anyone ever told you they would help you move and then didn't show up on moving day? Did you ever trust that per-son to come through on anything ever again??? Not likely. It doesn't take much for us to lose faith or not trust someone when they say they will do something and then don't follow through. It only takes one or two times for someone to flake out on us before we stop believing them. But why are we okay with lying to ourselves time and time again? You've got it. No one is there to hold us accountable.

About five years ago I announced on a conference call to a large group of people that I was going to write a book. For several months I would get questions. What kind of book is it, what's it about, yadi yada. Over time people stopped asking. More importantly they stopped believing. Then every now and again someone would ask how it was going or when I was going to finish it. I wanted to be honest so I said I hadn't even started. The day I quit my job I said I was quitting because I was going to write a book. Days turned into weeks, weeks turned into months and if I saw or heard from someone they asked if I had done it. And of course, I hadn't. The more time that went by, the longer it took, the less people believed me.

Are you going to talk or are you going to do? Do you say you're going to lose weight, quit smoking, stop drinking, get into shape? Do you do it? Words with no action are just words. Stop your talking and start doing. You have everything you need to get what you want. "I'm going to," can last a lifetime. Perhaps your intentions are good, but you just don't follow through. If you don't, you are lessening the value of your word and yourself. Don't just talk. Do.

Communicate what you want to yourself and others and communicate it in every form. You are far more likely to get what you want if you do.

The Third C is Create. Believe it or not, this is the easy part. You have already done the hard work. You thought it through, you planned out what needed to be done. If you started with the first C then you have already done the research and know what it is going to take to get what you want. If you weren't up for the challenge and weren't willing to do what it took to get to your goal, then you would have stopped there. So by now you've committed and communicated. You've told everyone you know what you are doing. Notice I said "doing", not going to do. You've written it down, you've signed a contract with yourself and you are surrounded by reminders of it every where you go. Now all you have to do is MAP it. Write down what needs to be done in the big picture. Then dice it up. Write down on your calendar every day the action you are going to take to get you one step closer. Before you know it you will be exactly who you want to be, have what you want to have, and have done what you wanted to do.

Commit, communicate, and create. It's as simple as 1,2,3 or C,C,C.

Follow the 3 C's to Succcess and you will Manifest Your Best.

Notes: What did I get out of this chapter? What do I want to remember? Etc.

_____

_____

_____

_____

_____

_____

_____

_____

_____

_____

_____

_____

_____

_____

_____

_____

_____

_____

Afterword

And those are the 7 Secrets to Create Your Fate. Everything you need is inside you. Every tool is at your disposal. The examples you have read are from real people just like you and me. Each of us has issues. Each of us has childhood garbage that doesn't really matter anymore. Each of us wish we had a better or a different upbringing. All of us have to deal with fear and stress. How you deal with it is what makes all the difference in the world.

On the next page I have shared a poem I wrote a few years ago. I wrote it when I was on vacation with several of my closest and dearest friends. Every time I have a bad day or am facing a challenge or need a little extra push in the right direction, I read it.

This poem will remind you of all that you are. It will remind you of all that you can do. It will remind you that it's all up to you.

I hope it empowers you as much as it has empowered me.

Reach for the stars.
Divine, complete, perfect that's what you are.

You can have what you want, sky is the limit.
Whatever it is, go out and get it.

Strive for the best, you deserve it all.
Make the choice, rise up high, and stand tall.

You've got the world in the palm of your hand.
Make a difference, aim high, take a stand.

Be strong, look in the mirror and love what you see.
When you dream, dream big, be all you can be.

Put the past behind you, forget all the strife.
Now is the time, take control of your life.

Have no fear, be courageous, you can do it, have no
doubt.
Today is the day, set your goals, make them count.

What is it that you want to achieve?
Trust me, its all in what you believe.

One thing to remember if you do you'll go far.
All you must do is reach for the stars.

If you aren't who you want to be, don't do what you want to do, or don't have what you want to have it is up to you to get it. There is no excuse now. You can no longer say, "I can't be, do, or have what I want." If you do, you're just lying to yourself. You are capable of anything. People have told me all my life that I have a desire that they don't or that I am more motivated. It's all an excuse to not take action. The only reason I have a desire for life or am motivated is because I know what I love and have passion for what I do and I live it every day.

I have done everything I am telling you to do. I have shared it with others and watched their hopes and dreams come true. I believe knowledge is power. If you give it away others will give it to you. Take what you have learned and act on it. Otherwise it is just useless information. Knowledge is nothing if you don't apply it.

I love my life. I love everything about it. Do you say the same? If there is something in my life that I don't love, I apply all the same tools that I have given you in this book. I ask myself the important questions. "What do I want?" It's not so much the answers that are important. It's the questions you are asking that really matter.

If you ask, "Why did this happen to me?" you will get the answer. Right, wrong or indifferent, it doesn't really matter. What difference does that answer make? It doesn't change the event. What happened, is simply...just what happened. The right answer to the wrong question, really is the wrong answer.

Better questions to ask are: "What did I learn from this?" "Can I grow and learn and be a better person?" "What do I want?" Those are the right questions. Ask yourself the right questions and you will get the right answers.

Thank you for giving me the opportunity to be a part of your life. As the philosopher Confucius said "The journey of a thousand miles begins with a single step." I truly hope this book has given you the tools, knowledge and inspiration to take that first step. Now apply what you have learned and Create Your Fate.

About the Author

Sharmen Lane is an inspirational writer, speaker and life coach. She has been a student of psychology for over 20 years and has trained, managed, and coached thousands of individuals on what it takes to get what one desires. She is currently completing her degrees in both psychology and communications. She published her first book, "Why Am I Special," for preschool age children in February 2006, which is a fully illustrated book that sends the message that all children are special, for no special reason. She currently has several seminars on her topics of Create Your Fate, The ABC's to Life, and The 3 C's to Success.

She was interviewed for the "America's Leadership Tribute" show produced by Sky Radio Network which will be broadcast on all American Airlines and US Airways flights worldwide starting October 6, 2006. The interview is to be nationally recognized in Newsweek magazine.

Sharmen inspires all that she comes in contact with to set their goals, live their passion and create their fate.

You can get more information on Sharmen's books, coaching programs and seminars on her website www. sharspeaks.com or by mail at SharSpeaks LLC, 2967 Michelson Drive, Suite G270, Irvine, Ca. 92612

Printed in the United States
204010BV00001B/1-105/A